Women in Space

REACHING THE LAST FRONTIER

Carole S. Briggs

Lerner Publications Company
Minneapolis

The jacket illustration shows Dr. Anna Fisher, astronaut, trying out the pilot position in the orbiter aeroflight simulator, or mission simulator, during a practice approach and landing situation.

The author would like to thank her editor, Theresa Early, for condensing and updating the manuscript.

For my mother, who's up there in spirit

This book is available in two editions:
Library binding by Lerner Publications Company
Soft cover by First Avenue Editions
241 First Avenue North
Minneapolis, Minnesota 55401

LIBRARY OF CONGRESS CATALOGING-IN-PUBLICATION DATA

Briggs, Carole S.
    Women in space: reaching the last frontier/Carole S. Briggs.
        p.   cm
    Includes index.
    Summary: Profiles the lives of many of the women who have been included in space programs in the United States, Russia, Canada, and Japan, describes their training, and highlights their achievements.
    ISBN 0-8225-1581-4 (lib. bdg.)
    ISBN 0-8225-9547-8 (pbk.)
    1. Women in astronautics—Juvenile literature. [1. Women astronauts. 2. Women in astronautics. 3. Astronautics.] I. Title.
TL793.B75 1988
629.45'0092'2—dc19
[920]   97-22919
                                                         CIP
                                                         AC

Manufactured in the United States of America

        4   5   6   7   8   9   10   98   97   96   95   94   93   92   91

Contents

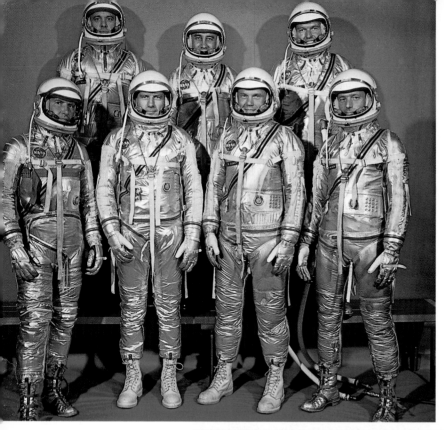

The first seven astronauts in the United States space program were chosen in April 1959. They were, front, left to right, Walter Schirra, Jr., Donald Slayton, John Glenn, Jr., and Scott Carpenter; back, Alan Shepard, Jr., Virgil (Gus) Grissom, and Gordon Cooper, Jr.

The first women astronauts in the United States space program were chosen in January 1978. Here they appear with a "rescue ball" (see pages 15-16). From left to right are Kathryn Sullivan, Rhea Seddon, Judith Resnik, Sally Ride, Shannon Lucid, and Anna Fisher.

A Giant Step for Womankind

"Three, two, one. Ladies and gentlemen, we have lift-off and America's first woman astronaut!" It was June 18, 1983. Amid the roar of two giant booster rockets and three powerful engines, Dr. Sally K. Ride and her crewmates shot up into outer space. Millions of women were at Cape Canaveral in body or in spirit, wishing her well, their hearts full of pride for what she represented. Women had climbed Mount Everest and dived 2,000 feet down into the ocean's depths. It was time to reach the final frontier—outer space.

A lot had changed since the Space Act of 1958 created the National Aeronautics and Space Administration (NASA). Back then only a small group of space projects existed: lunar probes,

a communications satellite, rocket engine research, and a brand-new project, the first man-in-space effort—Project Mercury. Six months after NASA was formed, the first seven United States astronauts were chosen.

At first, NASA was strongly committed to building new facilities. It built a research center for space satellites, Goddard Space Flight Center in Greenbelt, Maryland, and Johnson Space Center in Houston, Texas, and Cape Canaveral in Florida, which house the thousands of engineers and other flight personnel needed to put humans into space.

Project Mercury showed that the United States could launch a person into space and bring him safely home. Alan Shepard made the first trip in

1961. After a four-hour wait in a space capsule atop the Redstone rocket, Shepard's actual flight lasted only 15 minutes. It took a whole morning of television coverage to describe the flight, the landing of the capsule at sea, the recovery of the astronaut and his capsule, and his welcome back to earth by President John F. Kennedy.

As millions watch on television, *Friendship 7* lifts off with John Glenn aboard.

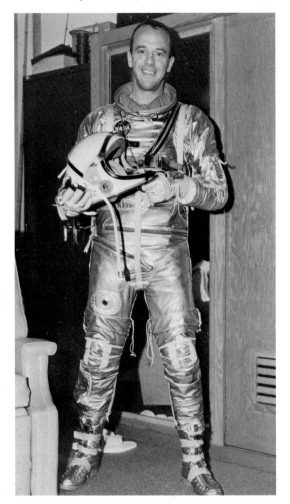

Alan Shepard in the pressure suit he wore for his historic flight

On February 20, 1962, millions again sat entranced in front of television sets as John Glenn, Jr., made the first flight all the way around the earth. He orbited the earth three times in *Friendship 7* during a five-hour flight. Everyone listened with awe as Glenn described the four sunsets he saw as he orbited. Announcer Walter Cronkite traced Glenn's path around the world, told what the inside of a space capsule was like, and explained the dangers of the intense heat of *reentry*.

A spacecraft goes outside earth's atmosphere on any trip into space. When it returns to earth, it has to reenter the atmosphere like a high diver entering a pool. The capsule is

moving at such a high speed that the air resists the capsule. Air rubs against the outside of a space vehicle so hard that the friction both slows the vehicle down and heats it up. Each spacecraft has special features which absorb or deflect the heat to keep the vehicle from burning up.

During the flight of *Friendship 7*, launch control received a signal that the capsule's heat shield was loose. If the heat shield came off during reentry, the capsule would burn up.

After the silence of reentry when no radio contact was possible with the space capsule, Glenn finally radioed to Houston: "Boy, that was a real fireball." A huge parade was held in New York City to celebrate the hero's safe return.

In 1962, a year before the end of Project Mercury, Project Gemini was begun. Nine more (male) astronauts were selected. Gemini would provide

Above: Wally Schirra's Mercury capsule is recovered from the ocean after his flight on October 3, 1962. **Below:** The Gemini astronauts stand on a launch pad at Cape Canaveral. **Left to right,** James McDivitt, John Young, Elliot See, Frank Borman, Edward White, Thomas Stafford, James Lovell, Charles Conrad, and Neil Armstrong

On June 3, 1965, *Gemini 4's* Ed White became the first United States astronaut to "walk in space." Behind him is the brilliant blue of the earth and its white cloud cover.

astronauts with the experience of living and maneuvering in space. Gemini astronauts would learn to *rendezvous with* and *dock*, or join, with another space vehicle. They would practice *extravehicular activity* (EVA) or moving around outside the space vehicle. Gemini was also the United States' first experience with sending two people aloft at once. Project Gemini prepared the United States to answer President Kennedy's challenge to land a man on the moon by the end of the 1960s.

Project Apollo took up the challenge. On July 16, 1969, *Apollo 11* set off for the moon. Four days later, the world heard astronaut Neil Armstrong say,

"Houston, Tranquility Base here. The *Eagle* has landed." And as he took his first steps on the lunar surface, he radioed home those famous words, "That's one small step for a man, one giant leap for mankind." Before the Apollo program ended, five more groups of astronauts explored the moon, collecting rock samples and carrying out experiments.

After the last Apollo mission to the moon came *Skylab*, an orbital workshop for long space missions. Three Apollo spacecraft were designed to dock with *Skylab*, a space laboratory. The plan was to launch *Skylab* empty, and then send up astronauts in an Apollo spacecraft to work in the lab.

Launch vibrations tore away *Skylab's* large sun shield, and at first NASA doubted whether the workshop could be used. For 10 hectic days the crew of the Apollo spacecraft worked to produce a makeshift sun shield. Then they docked with *Skylab* to conduct their experiments. Astronauts used *Skylab* for experiments in 1973 and 1974, and it fell to earth in 1979.

NASA scientists had always expected to work with scientists from other countries. In the first international venture, the Apollo-Soyuz Test Project (ASTP), a Soviet spacecraft docked with a U.S. spacecraft. Together, Soviet cosmonauts and United States astronauts conducted experiments in space science and life sciences.

The next generation of spacecraft was born in 1972 and is still in use — the space shuttle. NASA wanted a spacecraft that was reusable and would allow scientists from many countries to accompany their own experiments into space. Earlier spacecraft had been used only once and had splashed down into water at the end of a mission. The shuttle would take off like a rocket and land like an airplane, over and over. Not only would the shuttle save money because it could be reused, but since scientists would go along to conduct their own experiments, the pilots would not have to fly the craft and run the experiments as well. In this way, more experiments could be done at once.

On September 17, 1976, the first space shuttle, the *Enterprise*, was rolled

Astronaut Donald Slayton (bottom) and Cosmonaut Aleksey Leonov floated together in the *Soyuz* spacecraft during the Apollo-Soyuz Test Project in 1975.

out of the factory at Rockwell International in Palmdale, California. It was slowly pulled to Edwards Air Force Base in California where it was tested to ensure the safety of its crew. The first test the shuttle had to pass was the approach and landing test. NASA wanted to see which approach angles to the runway were best and also to get shuttle pilots used to guiding and landing their new aircraft. For these first tests, the shuttle used no engines. Instead, it was strapped to a Boeing 747 jumbo jet which took it up into the air. When the Boeing was high

The *Enterprise* rides a Boeing 747 carrier aircraft just before its first free flight test. Moments later the *Enterprise* separated from the 747 and made a short unpowered test flight.

enough, the shuttle was released and then flown in and landed like a glider.

After several glider-like flights, it was time to test the shuttle's powered flight. The shuttle has three main engines to push it along and two maneuvering nozzles which pilots use to move it around when it is in orbit. After the first engine test flight, its pilots pronounced the *Enterprise* a "great machine."

In 1978, the shuttle was attached to the rockets that would carry it into space. Its launching power comes from three rocket engines near its tail, which are fed from an external tank of liquid fuel, and two engines powered by solid-fuel rocket boosters. The external fuel tank is divided into two chambers, one containing liquid oxygen and one filled with liquid hydrogen. The solid rocket boosters simply boost the shuttle's takeoff power. They hold a rubbery fuel that burns at 560°F (295°C). Once the boosters are ignited, they burn until all of the fuel is spent. Several early unoccupied rockets exploded when this intense heat burned through a booster's outer casing.

NASA tested the shuttle's structural strength by subjecting it to vibrations which simulated lift-off. A space mission has the greatest potential for failure during launch. This is because of the tremendous force it takes to launch a vehicle into space. To lift a shuttle, the engines produce *thrust*, a pushing force. The force of thrust must be greater than the force of gravity in order to push the shuttle away from the earth. Together, the shuttle's five engines produce seven million pounds of thrust. This force could shake the shuttle and its fuel tanks apart if they were not properly designed or built.

Finally, the second shuttle orbiter,

Columbia, was declared ready for launching. The first shuttle flights would be called Space Transportation System (STS) flights. The first four flights, STS-1 through STS-4, were part of a program to test the shuttle and the astronauts. The rest of the shuttle missions would focus on tasks for government and private industry and on new devices placed on the shuttle.

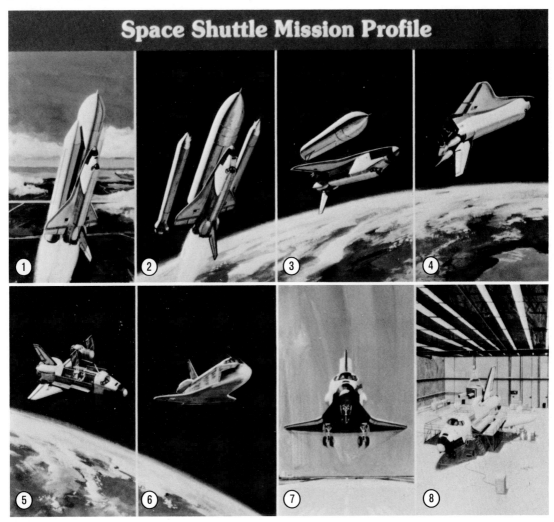

Space Shuttle Mission Profile

The stages of a shuttle mission: 1) take-off; 2) the solid rocket boosters run out of fuel and fall to earth; 3) the liquid fuel tank runs out of fuel and falls to earth; 4) the shuttle enters orbit; 5) the crew completes their operations; 6) the orbiter reenters the atmosphere; 7) landing; and 8) preparations for relaunch

Flight Crew

Shuttle flights have two pilots. One pilot acts as the *commander*. The commander controls the shuttle during launch, reentry, and in-flight maneuvers. The commander is also responsible for the overall success and safety of the flight. The other pilot—called the *pilot*—backs up the commander and may also help with experiments and with activities outside the shuttle (EVAs). The pilot and commander work for the National Aeronautics and Space Administration (NASA).

A pilot or commander must:

♦ have a bachelor's degree in engineering, physical science, life science, or mathematics (an advanced degree is preferred);

♦ have experience as a test pilot and at least 1,000 hours experience flying high-performance jet aircraft;

♦ be able to pass a tough physical examination;

♦ be between 5 feet 4 inches (1.6 m) and 6 feet 4 inches (1.9 m);

♦ have eyesight of 20/50 or better, uncorrected (correctable to 20/20).

Each flight also has several *mission specialists*. These crew members are responsible for planning in-flight activities. The mission specialists must understand the experiments to be done, the equipment used on board, and the kind of data to be collected. They might investigate the life cycle of the sun and stars. They might see if bees can fly when weightless, or they might test human blood circulation in zero gravity. They may also walk in space, use the shuttle's manipulator arm, and help launch and repair satellites. Mission specialists are trained as astronauts and work for NASA.

The requirements for mission specialists (both men and women) are slightly different than for pilot or commander. Mission specialists can be 5 feet (1.5 m) to 6 feet 4 inches (1.9 m) tall. Uncorrected eyesight must be 20/100 or better, correctable to 20/20. All of the women from the United States in the 1988 space shuttle program were mission specialists.

Accompanying the commander, pilot, and mission specialists on each shuttle flight might be a *payload specialist*. A *payload* is the cargo a spacecraft carries, including the scientific equipment used in experiments which take place during a mission. A payload specialist is usually a scientist who is familiar with the experimental equipment aboard the shuttle. Payload specialists are not trained by NASA as astronauts. Payload specialists may include astronomers, technicians who repair satellites in orbit, or even teachers. Women from all over the world will fly on the shuttle as payload specialists. Payload specialists spend from three to nine months working and training with NASA personnel before their flight.

The flight crew go through a training exercise at Johnson Space Center. Their seating pattern shows launch and landing positions.

Astronauts -in-Training

When NASA wants to add astronauts to its program, it advertises for applications. After it sorts through the flood of applications, it asks the most promising candidates to come to Johnson Space Center in Houston for interviews and examinations. Doctors ask the candidates detailed questions about their medical histories. Technicians measure their pulse rates during exercise to determine how strenuous a certain exercise is for them. To test for blood pressure problems or an irregular heartbeat, candidates jog uphill on a treadmill.

In one of the tests, candidates are sealed into spheres that force them to curl up in complete darkness. NASA personnel give them no idea how long they will be in there. If a shuttle were to become disabled, its crew would zip themselves up inside balls only

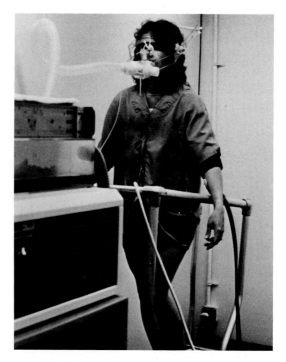

Payload specialist trainee Christa McAuliffe undergoes the treadmill stress test.

30 inches (76 cm) in diameter. These balls would protect them as they waited in their disabled shuttle in space for a rescue shuttle. When the rescue shuttle arrived, its crew would grab these balls by their handles and drop them into the new shuttle. The astronauts might be zipped into their "eggs" for several days before "hatching." For this reason, it is important that an astronaut does not fear being closed into a small, dark space.

Psychologists ask them questions, including "Do you love your mother?" and "If you were to die and come back as something other than human, what would it be?"

One of the doctors who interviews candidates told reporters what NASA seeks. The committee wants people with strong science backgrounds who have also done something extra. Because astronauts must perform a large variety of tasks, the ability to learn outside the original area of study is very important. So is the ability to set a goal and achieve it. Astronauts must be team players too, people who can work well with others.

Once an astronaut trainee is selected, she moves to the training facility in Texas, and the hard work begins. All new pilots and mission specialists train for one year. An astronaut must not only be familiar with her area of responsibility, she must also know how everything on the shuttle works in case a crew member becomes ill and she has to take on new duties very suddenly.

Astronaut trainees spend many hours in the classroom learning all aspects of the shuttle flight program. They take classes in flight mechanics, meteorology, rocket propulsion, computer science, upper atmosphere physics, astronomy, astrophysics, and aerodynamics. Their instructors come from the Johnson Space Center and from universities all over the world. There are no grades. They study hard simply because they want to learn all they can. Because there is so much training and expense involved, NASA asks all astronauts to sign a contract agreeing to work for them for seven years after the end of training.

Not only does the training period challenge the trainees' minds, but their physical strength is tested to the limit. For example, a new astronaut-in-training must learn to parachute from an airplane over both land and water, in case something happens to the shuttle. Trainees practice inflating and boarding life rafts and being lifted out of water by helicopter. On land, they may be required to spend three days surviving with only sleeping bags, pieces of parachute, and small survival kits containing dried food rations, a knife, and a fish hook.

Perhaps the most enjoyable aspect of their physical training is the experience of weightlessness. Some of the early astronauts and cosmonauts found it difficult to adjust to zero gravity in space. One way to avoid this problem is to allow astronauts to feel weightlessness before they go out

Above: Astronaut candidates, their training officer, and two physicians listen to a lecture. They include training officer Harold Ream and Rhea Seddon in row 1; Ellison Onizuka, Dr. Michael Berry, Jeffrey Hoffman and Ronald McNair in row 2; Anna Fisher (hidden), Kathryn Sullivan, George Nelson, and Steven Hawley in row 3; Judy Resnik (partly hidden), Sally Ride, Shannon Lucid, and Dr. Joseph DeGioanni in row 4. **Below:** Anna Fisher bobs in the water during survival tests.

Shannon W. Lucid floats aboard a KC-135 aircraft during zero gravity training.

into space. To let the trainees experience weightlessness, NASA takes them on special jet rides. The astronauts ride a KC-135 jet as it makes a series of arcs through the sky. Each arc begins with a steep climb and ends with a rapid descent. At the very top of an arc, the passengers become weightless for 30 seconds. This is barely enough time for the astronauts to practice moving around the cabin. Since trips in the KC-135 tend to produce motion sickness because of the swoops up and down, the astronauts have nicknamed it the "Vomit Comet."

Weightlessness can be simulated in water by SCUBA diving in a training tank. When the diver balances the forces against her so that the pressure of the water and of gravity pushing her down equal the pressure of the air in her vest pulling her up, she reaches neutral buoyancy. That means that she will neither float nor sink. This feels somewhat like weightlessness. All of the astronauts receive basic SCUBA training so that they can practice moving around in this kind of environment.

Pilot/astronauts spend 15 hours a

month flying T-38 trainer jets. Mission specialists ride in the rear seat of these supersonic jets and learn support skills like navigation, communications, and flight planning.

The astronaut also spends many hours in the mission simulator. A mission simulator is a model of the shuttle, complete with hundreds of switches, gauges, warning lights, and a window view. The astronaut "flies" this simulated shuttle under many different conditions. She learns what to do in emergency situations and practices docking with a space station and making a rendezvous with a satellite.

All astronauts are expected to keep physically fit. Many jog, several play racquetball, and all are encouraged to lift weights. It is important for an astronaut to be in good physical condition because muscles tend to lose their tone in space where they have no gravity to work against. The heart, the most important muscle, can lose its tone just like any other. In space, astronauts exercise on treadmills and bicycles to keep their hearts toned up, and they do stretching exercises for their other muscles.

After they are through with training, the astronauts are expected to work on other assignments for NASA and to keep up with their own special area of expertise. Physicians put in some hours in hospitals, for example, and engineers read journals and papers to keep up with research. An astronaut's assignment for NASA might be completely outside her former area of study. Some of the tasks NASA has assigned to astronauts include the redesign of the shuttle's toilet system and the writing of computer programs.

Once an astronaut is assigned to a mission, she works with the other members of her mission crew, rehearsing and preparing for the specific tasks the crew will be assigned.

Rhea Seddon "sits" down to a meal in the mid-deck of the space shuttle. Sleep restraints—"beds" with straps and zippers to keep the sleeper secure—are against the wall in the background.

Women in the United States Space Program

Until 1978, all of the astronauts chosen by NASA were male. With the shuttle program came the selection of NASA's first women astronauts. Women were finally admitted to the astronaut program for several reasons. A new law, a new space vehicle, and new attitudes all made a difference.

When NASA was formed in 1958, President Dwight D. Eisenhower, an army general himself, had ordered the agency to choose only military test pilots for the program. He reasoned that military pilots had several advantages for the astronaut program. Because they were in the military, the records of their training and experience were readily available. Military test pilots already had security clearances, and they could be ordered to Washington whenever they were needed. Because women are not allowed in combat, there were no female military test pilots—and therefore no female astronauts.

The military requirement was dropped for the second group of astronauts, chosen in 1962. Congress then ruled that admitting women to the space program would delay the United States' goal of putting a *man* on the moon before the end of the 1960s.

Finally, in 1972, Congress passed an amendment to the Civil Rights Act of 1964 stating that a federal agency cannot discriminate on the basis of sex, race, religion, or national origin. NASA is a federal agency, so it could not refuse to accept women.

The entry requirement was changed, and then NASA's program changed. Instead of one- or two-person missions, shuttle flights were planned to carry up to seven people. And the shuttle would go up more often than NASA's flights had gone up in the past—as often as one every two weeks. NASA might have 175 spaces to fill in the shuttle each year. A variety of specialists as well as pilots were needed in space. Leaving out highly qualified scientists and pilots who happened to be female did not make sense.

In 1977, NASA officials announced a need for new pilots and mission specialists. They received over 8,000 applications and asked 200 men and women to come to Johnson Space Center in Houston for physical examinations and interviews.

In January 1978, 15 people were selected as new pilot/astronauts, and 20 were named mission specialist/astronauts. Six of these mission specialists were women: Judith A. Resnik, Margaret Rhea Seddon, Anna L. Fisher, Shannon W. Lucid, Sally K. Ride, and Kathryn D. Sullivan. Two more female astronauts, Mary L. Cleave and Bonnie J. Dunbar, were added to the program as mission specialists in the second group of shuttle astronauts in 1980. All of these women flew in space before the shuttle program was interrupted by the tragedy in January 1986 which killed seven astronauts.

Other women astronauts are still awaiting their chance in space. Every

Mae C. Jemison became an astronaut candidate in 1987.

new list of astronauts now includes women. The class that joined in 1987 included Mae Jemison, the first black female astronaut.

Women have quickly fit into the space program. They undergo the same training and testing as the men. However, NASA had to build a women's locker room for the gymnasium at Johnson Space Center, and the seats in the

Astronaut trainees relax together during a break in survival class training. Ronald McNair is in front; others are George Nelson, Judy Resnik, Sally Ride, Kathy Sullivan, Rhea Seddon, Anna Fisher, and Shannon Lucid.

shuttle have been changed so they can be adjusted to women's shorter legs. The selection of personal gear that the astronauts can take along on the shuttle has been expanded to include tampons, skin moisturizers, and "hair restraints." Because working in a space suit on an EVA is especially tiring for a person's hands and arms, areas where women are often weaker than men, some of the women have found that they need to work to develop upper-body strength.

The Soviets and the Americans have both discovered a benefit to including women astronauts in their space programs. As the chief of the Soviet Cosmonaut Training Center has said, "We have noticed that in training and study, the whole work atmosphere and the mood in a crew of men and women are better than in men-only ones. Somehow, the women elevate relationships in a small team, and this helps to stimulate its capacity for work."

Vostok 6:
Valentina Tereshkova
First Woman in Space

On June 16, 1963, Russian cosmonaut Valentina Tereshkova was the first woman to go into space. Tereshkova had gone through months of training, including parachuting onto both land and water, keeping physically fit, training in an isolation chamber, and being whirled around in a centrifuge, a machine that simulates the effects of high gravity. She also trained as a pilot and practiced handling herself when weightless.

Her space capsule, *Vostok 6*, was very similar to the Mercury space capsules used by the United States except that it had an extremely heavy outer shell. *Vostok* weighed nearly five times Mercury's one-ton (907.2 kg) capsule.

Cosmonauts train for their flights in Star City outside Moscow. All spacecraft which carry cosmonauts are launched from Baikonur Cosmodrome in central Asia. Baikonur is nine times as large as Kennedy Space Center at Cape Canaveral. Soviet space activities are coordinated by the Soviet Academy of Sciences.

Tereshkova, or Valya as her family calls her, had wanted to be a cosmonaut for a long time. When Yuri Gagarin became the first man in space in 1961, Valya said that it was the most exciting day of her life. She loved the space program.

At the time of Gagarin's mission, Tereshkova was working as a cotton-spinning technologist at a cotton mill on the Upper Volga. She had made several parachute jumps in her free time and dreamed of nothing but going into space. When she felt she had perfected her jumping technique, she wrote to Moscow asking permission to train for space flight. A few months later she was asked to report to Star City to begin training. After working with her for several months, Gagarin said, "She was born for space."

On June 16, 1963, at 12:30 P.M., Tereshkova made world history. She blasted off the launch pad in *Vostok 6* to become the world's first spacewoman. Minutes after lift-off she came within three miles (five km) of Valery Fyodorovich Bykovsky, a cosmonaut who had been in orbit for two days in *Vostok 5*. Bykovsky had been scheduled to land when Tereshkova went up, but things were going so well that the Central Committee, which controls all space flights, decided that he should stay in space another three days.

As Tereshkova began her first orbit, she made radio contact with Bykovsky. "It's beautiful up here. I can see the horizon. What gorgeous colors," she said.

"I am sitting beside you. We are traveling through space side by side," Bykovsky radioed back. They sang a song together that evening to relax each other for sleep.

The next morning, Bykovsky could not raise his space companion. His radio messages went unanswered. Mission Control also tried, but their luck was no better. What could have happened to her? Finally, a sheepish voice came over the radio. Tereshkova had overslept.

On June 19, after three days in space, Tereshkova ejected herself from her capsule at a height of 4.2 miles (7 km) and parachuted to earth. Dozens of local people flocked around her to ask questions and to offer milk, cheese, and bread in case she was hungry.

By design, Tereshkova's flight had taken place one week before a worldwide conference on women was to be held in Moscow. The women at the conference took full advantage of the opportunity to celebrate her accomplishment. England's Queen Elizabeth wired her congratulations to Tereshkova.

Crowds in Moscow's Red Square carried portraits of Bykovsky, Tereshkova, and Lenin when they heard of Tereshkova's safe landing.

Above: Soviet cosmonauts and Premier Nikita Khrushchev wave from Lenin's Mausoleum in Red Square on June 22, 1963. Left to right, Pavel Popovich, Gherman Titov, Andrian Nikolayev, Yuri Gagarin, Valentina Tereshkova, Khrushchev, and Valery Bykovsky. **Right:** Tereshkova with husband Nikolayev and their daughter, Yelena

Six days later, Valery and Valentina were welcomed at Moscow's airport by Premier Nikita Khrushchev. They marched down a red carpet, he wearing his military uniform and she wearing a dark gray suit. Thousands of Russians were there cheering.

The two cosmonauts and the premier led a limousine procession to Red Square. The second limousine in the procession held four of the cosmonauts who had gone into space before them. Fourteen cosmonauts, four of them women, were present.

On November 3, 1963, Valentina Tereshkova married cosmonaut Andrian Nikolayev. Their little girl, Yelena, was born in 1964. Andrian and Valentina were the first pair of space travelers to have a baby after being exposed to the cosmic radiation of outer space. Apparently the radiation was not harmful, since Yelena was born without any health problems. After Yelena's birth, both Tereshkova and Nikolayev continued their cosmonaut training and their study of aircraft engineering.

A few years after her flight, Tereshkova won a seat on the U.S.S.R.'s powerful Central Committee. In 1983, she was honored on a new one-ruble coin. The engraving shows her in a space suit and helmet.

Above: The crew of the *Soyuz T-10* and *Soyuz T-12* inside *Salyut 7*. Svetlana Savitskaya is second from the right. **Below:** Savitskaya becomes the first woman to walk in space.

Soyuz T-7: Svetlana Savitskaya

On August 19, 1982, a crew of two men and one woman boarded *Soyuz T-7*, a capsule that was to be their home for eight days. The order was given to pull down their visors and fasten their shoulder straps. The huge booster rockets lifted them into space. Svetlana Savitskaya, a 34-year-old cosmonaut-researcher, sat between fellow cosmonauts Leonid Popov, the flight's commander, and Alexandr Serebrov. An experienced pilot, Savitskaya had broken the women's speed record for powered flight in 1975 and in 1980 she had won the women's world aerobatic championship. Still, she must have known that her life would never be the same after flying into space.

Savitskaya had been exposed to aircraft since her birth in 1948. Her father, Yevgeni Savitsky, held the very high rank of marshal of aviation. He

was a captain in the Soviet air force when World War II began. Captain Savitsky downed 22 German planes and was himself shot down 3 times. Once he even crawled from behind enemy lines with a fractured spinal column! By the end of the war he had flown 360 missions.

Svetlana Savitskaya became a student at the Moscow Aviation Institute and, when she was 15, forged her birth certificate to say she was 16 so that she could make her first solo flight. Her father pretended to know nothing about the flight before it happened, but he could not resist coming to the airfield to watch her solo. He was proud of his daughter's well-executed takeoff, flight, and landing. When she climbed out of the plane, he greeted her with a chocolate bar, the traditional flyer's ration. It meant that she was officially a pilot. By the time she was 17, Svetlana had set 3 world records in parachute jumping.

For the next 10 years Svetlana and her father both flew, often getting ready for flights together. When her father retired at age 64, Svetlana was an expert test pilot and well qualified to become a cosmonaut.

When she entered cosmonaut training, Savitskaya could fly 20 different planes and had also trained as a mechanical engineer. On the ground she helped design and test aircraft, but her role aboard the *Soyuz T-7* was a change from her "normal" duties. In space, she carried out various experiments in astrophysics and metallurgy as well as experiments on her body's reaction to weightlessness. During the eight-day flight, she also helped dock *Soyuz T-7* with *Salyut 7*, a space station that had been home to two other cosmonauts since May 1982. The crew left their *Soyuz T-7* capsule attached to *Salyut 7* and returned home on August 27, 1982, in the *Soyuz T-5*. The cosmonauts in *Salyut 7* would use *Soyuz T-7* to return home on December 7 after nearly eight months in space.

Salyut 7 still orbits the earth. In 1984, Savitskaya visited *Salyut 7* again, this time with crewmates Vladimir Dzhanibekov and Igor Volk in the *Soyuz T-12*. They were welcomed with gifts of bread and salt, Russian symbols of hospitality, by the four cosmonauts who had been living in *Salyut 7*

for several months. Savitskaya worked in space as she tested an arc welder outside the space station, becoming the first woman to perform an extra-vehicular activity.

Before her flight on *Soyuz T-12*, Savitskaya was asked how she felt about becoming the first woman to walk in space. She said, "A hundred years from now, no one will remember it, and if they do, it will sound strange that it was once questioned whether a woman should go into space."

The *Soyuz* spacecraft takes off from Baikonur Cosmodrome.

STS-7: Sally Ride,
First United States Woman in Space

Sally K. Ride stands in the mid-deck of the orbiting *Challenger*.

With a payload of two communications satellites and seven "getaway specials," canisters containing various experiments, the space shuttle *Challenger* soared into the heavens. On board was Dr. Sally Ride, the United States' first female astronaut. It was June 18, 1983.

Ride commented, "You spend a year training just which dials to look at and when the time comes, all you want to do is look out the window. It's so beautiful."

Ride acted as flight engineer for this seventh shuttle flight, STS-7. That meant that she was responsible for ensuring that the shuttle's mechanical systems were performing properly. She had to understand each of the instruments on the flight deck and explain any indicated problems to commander Robert Crippen.

In addition, Ride and fellow mission specialist John Fabian were to *deploy,*

The STS-7 crew included Robert L. Crippen (front row, center), commander; Frederick Hauk (right), pilot; and Sally K. Ride, John Fabian, and Norman Thagard, mission specialists.

or place in position, two satellites. The *Anik C-2* communications satellite belongs to Canada. The *Palapa B-2* is a communications satellite belonging to the telecommunications company that ties together Indonesia's 3,000 islands. The satellites were carried in the shuttle's *cargo bay*, a large compartment at the rear of the shuttle that opens into space.

NASA was paid to deploy these satellites by the satellites' owners. Many of the astronauts' duties on shuttle missions are experiments or tasks which they do for paying customers of NASA. The income from these tasks helps pay the costs of training, equipment, fuel, and research for the space program.

After seven orbits, Ride and Fabian prepared the *Anik* satellite for deployment. Twenty minutes later *Challenger's* on-board computer decided that the space shuttle was in the correct spot. The computer exploded the clamps that held *Anik* in the cargo bay and, using powerful springs, pushed the satellite out of the cargo bay. The satellite's own motor later adjusted its position and speed so that it assumed a proper orbit. Ride and Fabian repeated this procedure to deploy the Indonesian satellite.

Ride and Fabian also worked with the remote manipulator system (RMS), later named the Canadarm, which they and several Canadian engineers designed. The remote manipulator system is a robotic arm. It bends in the middle, like a human elbow does, and its "hand" is designed to grasp satellites. The Canadarm extends into the cargo bay, but the person operating it stays inside the shuttle. The operator can see where the arm is and what it is doing via a television camera. The RMS can be used to pluck satellites out of storage in cargo bay and ready them for launch, to help build space structures, and to do anything outside the cockpit.

On June 22, Fabian used the RMS to lift the German *Shuttle Pallet Satellite (SPAS)* from the cargo bay into space. *SPAS* carried eight experiments ranging from the measurement of solar-cell characteristics to how different alloys mix in zero gravity. It floated up to a half mile above the *Challenger* for more than 10 hours. Then Ride used the RMS to retrieve *SPAS* and the experiments.

While she was retrieving *SPAS*, *Challenger*'s small control rockets were fired. This tested the effects of movement on the arm while it was extended.

After six days in space, *Challenger* was to be the first shuttle to land where it took off, at Kennedy Space Center. This would save the shuttle the expensive, week-long trip from its landing site back to the Cape to

A cutaway view of a space shuttle's crew compartment. The crew are at work stations in the upper flight deck. Below them is the mid-deck where they eat, sleep, and conduct some experiments.

be readied for the next flight. Unfortunately, bad weather forced them to land at Edwards Air Force Base, where the other shuttle flights had landed. President Ronald Reagan joked to commander Crippen that "You didn't stop and pick me up off the South Lawn [of the White House] like I asked you to."

Both the most fun and the hardest part of being in space, Sally Ride commented, was the experience of weightlessness. It was fun to walk on walls and ceilings, but she felt frustrated by the clumsiness that weightlessness brings on. "It will take you 10 minutes just to open your clothes locker," she said. "You don't really bump into things but you don't know how to control your body, so your legs go flailing in one direction and your arms in another."

Sally Ride trained all her life to be able to control her body—and her mind—in space. She was born on May 26, 1951, in Los Angeles. She thought for many years that she would become a professional athlete. She played softball and football and then discovered tennis at the age of 10. In her teens, she was a nationally ranked amateur tennis player. By her senior year at Westlake High, she was captain of the tennis team. At age 22, while Ride was attending Stanford University, tennis pro Billie Jean King saw Ride play. King advised her to leave Stanford and become a professional tennis player, but Ride decided to keep on with her studies.

School was always easy for Ride, and she loved math and science. At Stanford, she chose to study for a Ph.D. in astrophysics. Astrophysicists study the makeup and evolution of the stars and the light they give off. She was a member of a research team that studied high-energy lasers.

A doctorate (Ph.D.) in any science takes a long time to earn. Five years is about average. The time is spent mostly in doing research on a very specific topic in the student's field. The student poses several detailed questions and then runs experiments to try to find the answers. Sometimes an experiment that a scientist has worked on for months gives unclear results or fails altogether, so the experiment has to be redesigned and begun again. The last year of work on a Ph.D. is usually spent writing a dissertation, a lengthy description of the research and what can be learned from it. Sally finished hers in 1978.

Sally also joined NASA in 1978. One of her assignments for NASA was as a capsule communicator (*capcom*) for STS-2 and STS-3. The capcom is an astronaut who talks to the shuttle crew from ground control while the shuttle is in space. Her job is to relay messages from the technicians at Johnson Space Center to the shuttle. The capcom is often called "the voice of Mission Control." A capcom must understand everything that goes on during a flight. She must stay calm, and her instructions must be clear and precise because the life of the crew is

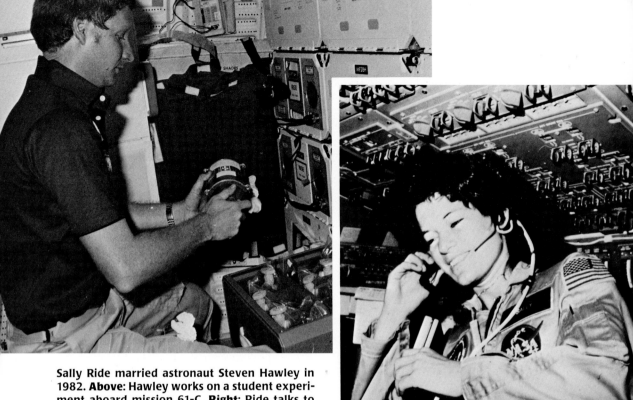

Sally Ride married astronaut Steven Hawley in 1982. **Above:** Hawley works on a student experiment aboard mission 61-C. **Right:** Ride talks to ground controllers during STS-7.

at stake. The job of capcom rotates through the astronaut corps.

In July 1982, Sally Ride, dressed in blue jeans and sneakers, married fellow astronaut Steve Hawley. They lived near Houston in Clear Lake City, a town full of NASA technicians, engineers, astronauts, and their families.

Once it was announced that Sally Ride would become the first woman NASA sent into space, Ride became a celebrity. She was interviewed for newspapers and magazines, television shows and radio shows. She does not like being a celebrity just because she is an astronaut who happens to be female. She considers herself a scientist, not a *female* scientist. She did admit to being flattered—but embarrassed—when the people of Woodlands, Texas, voted to name their elementary school Sally K. Ride Elementary School.

Ride left NASA in 1987 to take up a post at Stanford University. She left behind a record of achievement and accomplishment at NASA. Sally Ride became a model for women to look up to when she became an astronaut. Tamara Jernigan, who joined the space program in 1985, told one reporter that "Her (Ride's) acceptance as a mission specialist . . . made me realize I had a chance at becoming an astronaut."

Mission 41-D: Judith Resnik

The orbiter *Discovery* lifted off from Kennedy Space Center on August 30, 1984, at 8:41 A.M. EDT. This was the first launch for *Discovery* and also the first time Judith Resnik had flown on the shuttle.

The six-day mission was going to be a very busy one for Resnik and her five crewmates. Mission 41-D had been scrubbed (postponed) twice since June 26 because of engine problems. The most important payload items were put aboard *Discovery*. It carried the heaviest payload in the shuttle's history, 47,000 pounds (21,150 kg).

About eight hours into the mission, *SBS-D*, a communications satellite, was deployed. Resnik and her crewmates watched in fascination as the

The gold-colored solar panel for the *OAST-1* stands out against the darkness of space.

The crew of mission 41-D leaves the launch pad after a countdown test. Leading is pilot Michael Coats, followed by mission specialist Judith Resnik, commander Henry Hartsfield, mission specialist Mike Mullan, and payload specialist Charles Walker.

huge cylinder spun away from the cargo bay into the heavens. Two more communications satellites were deployed on the second and third days.

Discovery also carried the *OAST-1* solar wing, which is 13 feet (3.9 m) wide, extends to a height of 102 feet (30.6 m), and folds into a package only 7 inches (17.5 cm) deep. On this wing were several types of solar cells. The *Discovery* crew unfolded and refolded the wing several times to test its durability and the functioning of the solar cells. The orbiter's *vernier*

engines, the small engines it uses to maneuver in orbit, were fired while the wing was unfolded so that the astronauts could observe the wing's movement and vibration under stress.

Discovery touched down at Edwards Air Force Base on September 5, 1984. In spite of the busy schedule, the crew had met most of the goals for the flight. This kind of schedule was perfect for Judith Resnik, who had said that "I like making a contribution to one project and then moving on to something else."

38

Born in Akron, Ohio, on April 5, 1949, Judith Resnik (J.R. to her friends) was an extremely able student. She took piano lessons and became so good at it that she considered a career as a concert pianist. However, she loved nothing better than a long series of complicated math problems. She took school seriously, determined to learn as much as she could.

She worked her way through Carnegie-Mellon University, receiving her bachelor's degree in electrical engineering in 1970. She went to work for RCA Corporation, first in the missile and surface radar division and then in the service division. Resnik left RCA in 1974 to become a staff scientist in the neurophysiology laboratory at the National Institutes of Health.

Continuing her schooling at the University of Maryland, she received her Ph.D. in electrical engineering in 1977. She was hired as a product developer for Xerox Corporation.

As soon as she heard that NASA was willing to admit women to the space program, she was determined to become an astronaut. She began a program to improve her odds of being chosen. She ran regularly to get into better physical shape and visited the National Air and Space Museum in Washington and learned everything she could about NASA. She talked to her congressional representative and even took flying lessons. Obviously, something worked. She joined the space program in 1978.

In 1982, Judith Resnik appeared on ABC News to explain what was happening on board the fourth shuttle mission. She also worked with Sally Ride on the design and development of the remote manipulator system. Judith Resnik was one of the group of astronauts killed in the explosion of the *Challenger* on January 28, 1986. She will be sorely missed.

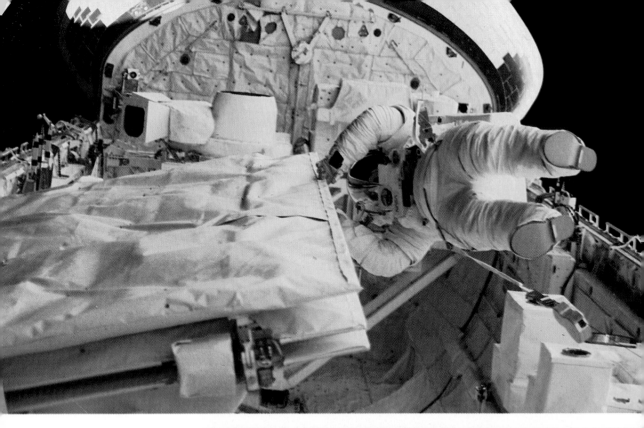

Above: Kathryn Sullivan checks the *SIR-B* antenna during her historic EVA on October 11, 1984. She was America's first woman to walk in space. **Right:** The RMS holds *Earth Radiation Budget Satellite (ERBS)* ready for launching during mission 41-G.

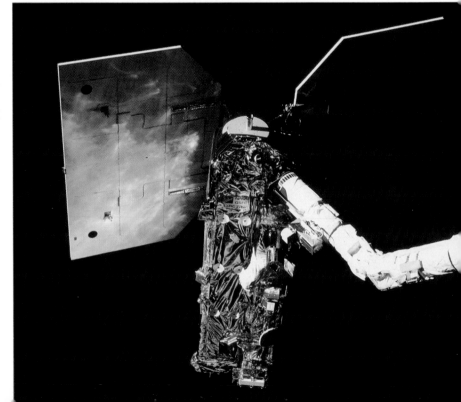

Mission 41-G: Kathryn Sullivan

Mission 41-G, the sixth launch for *Challenger* and the thirteenth space shuttle mission, was to be full of firsts. It was the first flight to have two women aboard (Sally Ride and Kathryn Sullivan), the first mission to have seven crew members, the first to have a Canadian aboard (Marc Garneau), the first space walk by an American woman (Sullivan), the first to include an astronaut on his fourth mission (Robert Crippen), and the first demonstration of refueling a satellite to extend its life.

Challenger lifted off from the Kennedy Space Center on October 5, 1984. Less than nine hours into the mission, the *Earth Radiation Budget Satellite (ERBS)* was lifted out of cargo bay. *ERBS* measures the amount of energy the earth receives from the sun and radiates back into space and the movement of energy on the earth. It will help meteorologists predict weather patterns more accurately.

Next, the crew activated the *Shuttle Imaging Radar-B (SIR-B)*. The *SIR-B* was supposed to collect data from a satellite already in orbit and relay that data to earth. The radar worked, but a problem with the shuttle's antenna left the *SIR-B* unable to *track*, or keep its instruments aligned to receive a signal. The crew locked the antenna in place and then turned the shuttle so that the antenna was always pointed at the satellite in orbit. This maneuver is like turning your house instead of the TV antenna to get better reception.

Because of the problems with *SIR-B*,

The crew of mission 41-G: left to right, pilot Jon McBride, payload specialist Paul Scully-Power, Sally Ride, commander Robert Crippen, Kathryn Sullivan, payload specialist Marc Garneau, representing the National Research Council of Canada, and mission specialist David Leestma

the space walk by Kathryn Sullivan and David Leestma had to be delayed for two days. Finally, on October 11, Sullivan became the first American woman to walk in space. Moving and working in open space, she and Leestma tested ways to refuel satellites in orbit. Satellites that have run out of fuel are useless, because they can no longer relay signals or radio information to earth. They need fuel to run their transmitters and receivers. If satellites could be refueled rather than replaced, NASA and its customers could save billions of dollars. The two mission specialists spent over

three and a half hours in the *Challenger's* cargo bay attaching a refueling line to a tank filled with fuel for the satellite. The refueling system was checked several times and worked well. Sullivan and Leestma proved that it was possible and practical to refuel satellites in orbit.

Dangling at a 90° angle to the spacecraft, Sullivan and Leestma also aligned the frozen antenna so that it could be firmly attached and operated from inside the cabin. After several suggestions by commander Crippen that Sullivan and Leestma return to the cabin, the astronauts finally ended their space walk. "No sweat," Kathy Sullivan said, smiling, as she floated inside.

The astronauts also took detailed photographs of the earth. They used a large-format camera that can photograph something as small as a house —in detail—from space, and another camera that measures the distribution of air pollution over the entire planet.

The crew also measured the amount of radiation outside the shuttle in an experiment developed by the Central Research Institute for Physics in Budapest, Hungary. Payload specialist Garneau performed medical, atmospheric, climatic, materials, and robotics experiments for Canada. Paul Scully-Power, the other payload specialist, performed a series of oceanography experiments.

Challenger landed at Kennedy Space Center on October 13. The flight had lasted 8 days, 5 hours, and 23 minutes.

Born in Patterson, New Jersey, on October 3, 1951, Kathryn Sullivan holds a B.S. in earth science from the University of California at Santa Cruz and a Ph.D. in geophysics from the University of Dalhousie, Halifax, Nova Scotia. She spent one year as an undergraduate exchange student at the University of Bergen in Norway. She learned Norwegian before she went, one of six languages she has mastered. Ideally, Sullivan says, she'd like to learn everything there is to learn.

She joined NASA because of her love of knowledge and exploration.

That is also the reason she specialized in marine geology—77 percent of the earth is covered by water, so there is a lot to learn and explore.

At first she laughed when her brother showed her a newspaper advertisement asking for astronaut applicants. Why would NASA want a marine geologist? But she read more about the position in some of her science magazines. She realized that flying on the space shuttle would not be so different from sailing on marine research vessels, as she had already done. She knew how to communicate with a research base, to navigate without landmarks, and to live and work in cramped quarters with other people.

For others who want to become involved in space exploration, she recommends that they realize what it takes to set a goal and work toward it. She says that as an explorer you must believe in yourself, pick the thing you excel in and make the most of the opportunities in that area. She knows firsthand that it takes patience and dedication. Astronaut training and the work of astronauts is mostly a matter of self-discipline. "Nobody sits on you to make sure you work from eight to four. It's 'Get the job done.'"

Anna Fisher trains for her space trip in an extravehicular mobility unit (space suit).

Mission 51-A: Anna Fisher

The sun had not yet peeked over the horizon, and it was just beginning to paint the sky with its orange light. But the day was already well underway at Kennedy Space Center. Five on-board computers noiselessly checked and rechecked *Discovery's* systems in an attempt to ensure a safe flight. The area was cleared of all but emergency personnel as five astronauts approached the orbiter. Dressed in blue jumpsuits, they waved at the television cameras and at the excited crowd in the viewing area. The crew were preparing to board. It was November 8, 1984.

Once on board the crew began its preflight check of the vehicle. The countdown reached its end. Flames flashed from the shuttle's base, and smoke and steam billowed from the launch pad. With an earthshaking tremble and a gigantic roar, *Discovery* shot to an altitude of 500 feet (150 m) in 3 seconds. The orbiter arced over the Atlantic Ocean, turning on its back. Anna Fisher and her crewmates were pressed into their seats by a force of three *Gs*. This means the acceleration of the shuttle was pressing on them with a force three times as great as gravity on earth.

The solid rocket boosters stopped firing when they ran out of fuel, 27 miles up. They dropped away from the shuttle and their parachutes unfolded, slowing them down so that they could land safely and be used again. *Discovery's* engines continued to burn liquid fuel and took the orbiter to a height of

The crew of 51-A included Frederick Hauk, front, as commander, and mission specialist Dale Gardner, pilot David Walker, and mission specialists Anna Fisher and Joseph Allen.

over 100 miles (62 km). The crew and their cargo were travelling about 17,500 miles per hour (27,900 kph). The earth's gravity no longer weighed them down—the astronauts became weightless. Now the work for which the crew had trained for a year began.

NASA had made a three-part effort to show off the capabilities of the shuttle program. Part one was mission 41-C's repair of a satellite in space and part two was mission 41-G's satellite-refueling experiments. Mission 51-A would show that satellites could be recovered from orbit and taken back to earth for repairs.

Two communications satellites were launched on the second and third days of the mission. That made room in the cargo bay for the satellites that needed repairs.

On the fifth day of the mission, *Discovery* fired its rockets in preparation for rendezvous with the first of the two satellites that needed repairing.

Joseph Allen and Dale Gardner went into the cargo bay to capture the satellite. They held it steady while Fisher used the RMS to pull the satellite into the cargo bay. Gardner tried to attach a special bridge to the satellite that would enable Fisher to lock it into its berth. Unfortunately, the bridge did not fit. Allen held the satellite steady for two hours while Gardner prepared it for berthing in the cargo bay. By sheer force, the two astronauts finally seated the satellite in its cradle. They repeated this procedure to capture and berth the other satellite the next day.

Commander Frederick Hauk landed *Discovery* on November 16 after a flight of 7 days, 23 hours, and 45 minutes. Fisher smiled at the cheering crowd as she came down the steps leading from the orbiter to the landing strip. She was the first mother to fly in space.

When Anna Fisher started the astronaut training program, she did not even know how to put on a parachute,

The shuttle flies above the earth with an open cargo bay. The RMS is visible on the left.

much less fly an airplane. Now putting on a parachute is easy, and she spends hours aboard NASA's T-38 trainer jets or flying in a Cessna 150.

Fisher had majored in chemistry at the University of California at Los Angeles (UCLA). She chose medicine because she thought it would help her become an astronaut. As she said, "When I was young I thought about being an astronaut. But I didn't know how to go about it. There were no women in my field until 1978 [when the first women joined the astronaut training group]. There were, however, women in medicine, and I did think that someday doctors would be needed on space stations, so that's the route I took."

Before she decided on medical school, Fisher seriously studied both ballet and gymnastics. However, once in medical school at UCLA, she found that she liked team sports—so she organized a women's basketball league. She also learned to enjoy water polo.

Anna met her husband Bill when both were in medical school. Like Anna, Bill was training in emergency room care. Emergency room care is a new field that requires a broad knowledge of medical and surgical techniques, the ability to make the right decisions under the pressure of a crisis, and frequent 24-hour shifts.

Anna and Bill were married in 1977. Both applied to the astronaut training program as soon as they heard about it. Anna was accepted as an astronaut trainee in 1978—before Bill was. He

47

After landing, Anna Fisher meets the press with her husband, Bill Fisher, and Kristin Anne.

was both disappointed and delighted. They moved to Texas so that Anna could begin training. Bill was accepted into the astronaut program two years later with another group of shuttle astronauts. Their daughter Kristin Anne was born in 1983.

As a physician, Fisher has some very special concerns about space flight. One of her projects is research into the problems of calcium loss and brittle bones that astronauts, especially women, run into when they are weightless.

For the first flight of the space shuttle *Columbia* in 1981, Anna Fisher was stationed at an alternate landing site in White Sands, New Mexico. She was on hand as a medical expert in case something went wrong.

As part of her training for that mission, Fisher had been sent to San Diego for a conference on emergency medicine. There she had heard lectures about topics such as what to do if one of the shuttle's fuels gets on someone's skin and how to move an injured person out of the orbiter.

Fisher also worked on the tile repair kit. Each shuttle is coated with more than 30,000 ceramic tiles that insulate it against the heat of reentry. These tiles can reach 2750° F (1510° C). Fisher helped design a kit that astronauts could use to replace lost tiles while in space.

Fisher says that being away from her daughter was the hardest part of her shuttle flight. Every astronaut spends several days in preflight quarantine in addition to his or her time in space, so mission 51-A took her away from Kristin for about two weeks. Fisher feels that there are benefits for Kristin. She will grow up thinking that it is normal to have astronaut parents and will not feel as if some jobs are closed to women.

Mission 51-D: Margaret Rhea Seddon

The crew of mission 51-D had a busy schedule. Due to mechanical problems with earlier flights, the crew's original payloads were put on another flight. The crew had been assigned a new mission, and on April 12, 1985, they were finally aboard *Discovery*, awaiting lift-off.

Nine hours and forty-five minutes after lift-off, the crew successfully deployed an *Anik* satellite for Canada. Rhea Seddon conducted some experiments to study how the heart pumps blood in zero gravity.

The next major task was deploying an $85 million satellite called *Leasat* for the U.S. Navy. *Leasat* had been designed to be deployed without first being checked by the astronauts. This proved to be a disadvantage. Shortly after *Leasat* was put into orbit, Seddon observed that its antenna had not come up. A lever was supposed to pop

During zero-gravity training on the KC-135, Rhea Seddon "lifts" astronaut Robert Gibson. The two were married in May 1981.

The seven members of the 51-D mission crew are, front row, commander Karol Bobko, pilot Donald Williams, and mission specialists Rhea Seddon and Jeffrey Hoffman; back row, mission specialist David Griggs and payload specialists Charles Walker and Senator Jake Garn of Utah.

into position and turn *Leasat*'s electrical power on when the satellite left the cargo bay. Apparently this arming lever had jammed.

Back on earth, NASA astronauts and engineers talked about different ways to solve the problem. Some astronauts went into a water tank with another *Leasat* and used various tools to see what might work to loosen the lever. Others climbed into the shuttle simulator to plan *Discovery*'s rendezvous with *Leasat* and to see how the manipulator arm might be used in the repairs.

At the same time, astronauts and technical crew were debating whether *Discovery* should even try to repair the

satellite. After all, no one knew exactly what the problem was, and the satellite did carry six tons of very flammable fuel. It could be dangerous for the astronauts to go near it again. The longer the satellite neither exploded nor turned itself on, however, the safer it seemed to be. Preparations went on for the repairs.

Finally, late on April 14, flight director Larry Bourgeois and his team designed devices that could be used to snare the lever. A team of astronauts led by Sally Ride built the snares from materials that would be on board *Discovery*, in order to make sure that the *Discovery* crew could build them.

Then Ride's team practiced snaring the lever on their *Leasat*. They worked around the clock to perfect a method, and then radioed instructions to *Discovery*. On April 16, shuttle astronauts David Griggs and Jeffrey Hoffman donned space suits for the first unplanned space walk in the history of the United States space program. Within an hour they had the snare attached to the RMS. Seddon practiced moving the manipulator arm around the cargo bay with the snare on its end.

Very early on April 17, Karol Bobko and Donald Williams used the rendezvous procedures which had been

Top: Rhea Seddon cuts out the pieces which will go into the snare to be used on *Leasat*. **Bottom left**: She holds the finished "lacrosse stick" snare. **Right**: The lacrosse stick is attached to the end of the RMS.

radioed to them. They brought *Discovery* within 35 feet of *Leasat*. Seddon began to move the snare into position. She succeeded in moving the stubborn lever three times. She even hit it once, just to make sure. It was all in vain, however: *Leasat*'s electrical system still failed to function. Apparently, the arming lever was not the problem after all. Disappointed and tired, the crew landed on April 19.

Margaret Rhea (pronounced *ray*) Seddon was born on November 8, 1947, in Murfreesboro, Tennessee. She wanted to be an astronaut since she was 14. That was the year Alan Shepard became the first astronaut from the United States to be shot into space. Although none of the astronauts in the program then were women, Rhea believed that some day women would be admitted to the space program. She was determined to be ready.

She knew that any astronaut accepted for the program would need very special qualifications. Rhea decided that her special contribution would be to become a physician. In high school she took math and science courses and worked hard at them. Both her parents supported her struggle.

Her friends did not. They thought she would be so busy being a "brain" that she would never get married. Seddon, however, was undaunted. She enjoyed being a cheerleader, joined the Girl Scouts and Thespians, was a member of the school newspaper staff, the science club, the Mathematics Honor Society, National Honor Society, and Latin club.

Rhea Seddon graduated from high school in 1966 and enrolled as a pre-med (pre-medical school) student at the University of California at Berkeley. The first year was a great shock. The university was large and very competitive. One-third of the class would not make it to the second year. Seddon knew her grades were just not good enough to get her into medical school. Maybe, she thought, she should give up on becoming a doctor. She went back to Tennessee and enrolled in a nursing program at Vanderbilt University.

But her desire to be an astronaut would not leave her. After a year, Seddon returned to Berkeley, determined to study hard and get into medical school. She graduated with honors.

Seddon received her undergraduate degree in physiology from Berkeley. She then went to medical school at the University of Tennessee at Memphis. During her internship and residency, she became interested in a specialty of medicine called surgical nutrition. This involves the special feeding of patients who have had major surgery.

In 1975, between her internship and her residency, Seddon decided that a pilot's license would increase her chances of becoming an astronaut. Working nights in hospital emergency rooms, she took flying lessons during the day. Within several months, she had her pilot's license.

When the announcement came from NASA in 1977 that they would be accepting applications from both men and women for the shuttle program, Rhea Seddon was ready to apply. She was thrilled when she was asked to come to Houston for a series of physical exams and interviews.

Seddon returned to Veterans Hospital in Memphis to finish her residency and await NASA's decision. On January 16, 1978, George Abbey, director of flight operations at Johnson Space Center, called to ask if Dr. Seddon would like to become a trainee for the astronaut corps. Would she! Her delighted co-workers nicknamed her "Cosmic Rhea."

Astronaut trainee Seddon moved to Texas. She became one of more than 20,000 NASA employees at the Johnson Space Center. Like all trainees, Seddon learned to parachute through trees and power lines and into water. She lifted weights, ran, and took classes in astronomy, shuttle design, geology, engineering, and computers. At the end of 12 months she was an astronaut.

Because of her interest in nutrition, shuttle food became one of her specialties. Seddon also helped design *payload software*, the computer programming needed for various experiments done aboard the space shuttle.

Her talents as a doctor were also put to use. She helped find a way to perform artificial respiration and cardiopulmonary resuscitation on a person in space. During zero gravity training in the KC-135 jet, she experimented with resuscitation techniques on a large doll. To Rhea's frustration, it kept floating away from her when she tried to push down on its chest or to breathe into its lungs. Finally, Seddon and some of the other mission specialists devised a restraint that allows a rescuer to push up against the victim with her legs.

On May 30, 1981, Dr. Rhea Seddon married Robert Lee (Hoot) Gibson, an astronaut and former navy fighter pilot. They met during their training and became the first astronauts to marry. In 1982, their son Paul was born.

Says Seddon of her work with NASA, "I don't think a day goes by when I don't learn 10 new things. That's my favorite part about being in the program. I'm probably going to remain an astronaut for a long time. I want NASA to get its money back for my training."

The mission 51-G crew pose for a portrait. In front are commander Daniel Brandenstein and pilot John Creighton. Behind them stand mission specialists Shannon Lucid, Steven Nagel, and John Fabian, and payload specialists Prince Sultan bin Salman bin Abdul Aziz of Saudi Arabia and Patrick Baudry of France.

Mission 51-G: Shannon Lucid

The date: June 17, 1985. NASA's orbiter *Discovery* had once again soared into the heavens.

In addition to deploying three communications satellites (for Mexico, the Arab countries, and the United States) and conducting some getaway specials, mission 51-G had two main goals. The first was to test the accuracy of a low-energy laser beam. The second was to deploy *Spartan 1*, a free-flying platform that would study the central core of the Milky Way galaxy.

On June 21, while the orbiter was in darkness during its 64th orbit, a low-energy laser beam was directed from Hawaii to *Discovery*. Researchers at the United States Air Force Optical Station on Maui located *Discovery* with radar as it flew about 200 nautical miles (230 land miles or 368 km) overhead. *Discovery*'s crew also lit a one-million-candlepower docking light in the left flight deck window to help the scientists spot them from below. Personnel on Maui "zapped" *Discovery* with a laser beam, pretending that it was an "enemy" rocket. The beams bounced off a reflector on the orbiter and were received by detectors on Maui.

At its source, the laser beam had a diameter of 0.25 inches (.52 cm). By the time it illuminated *Discovery*, the beam was 30 feet (9 m) across.

Shannon Lucid used the RMS to deploy *Spartan 1*. *Spartan 1* studied the Perseus cluster of galaxies and the central core of the Milky Way. It flew free of the shuttle for 45 hours and

Shannon Lucid joins Patrick Baudry (in front) and John Creighton in experiments on the human body.

recorded data for 24 hours during 16 orbits of the earth.

During the seven-day mission, French payload specialist Patrick Baudry also conducted experiments on the heart and on how the body positions itself in space. French and Russian scientists had discovered in 1982 on the Russian space lab, *Salyut 7*, that vision is important in helping the body adjust to a weightless environment. They also learned that blood flows faster near the heart during weightlessness but not in the rest of the body. Baudry's experiments were designed to add to this knowledge.

Lucid and Prince Sultan bin Salman bin Abdul Aziz of Saudi Arabia helped with these experiments, and the Prince also conducted experiments designed by Arab scientists.

Discovery touched down at Edwards Air Force Base on June 24, 1985.

Dr. Shannon Wells Lucid was born in Shanghai, China, in 1943. Her parents were in China as Baptist missionaries. The Wellses were taken prisoner by the Japanese when Shannon was six weeks old. When she was one, they were allowed to return to the United States. After World War II, her parents went back to China, only to be expelled by the Communists in 1949. The Wellses moved to Lubbock, Texas, and later to Bethany, Oklahoma, the family's original hometown.

Shannon graduated from Bethany High School and went to Wheaton College in Illinois. She got a good grounding in chemistry there, but she was just barely able to pay her way. She worked in the student union and cleaned houses in order to earn her fees. Then Wheaton raised its fees, so she switched to the University of Oklahoma in Norman. She earned her B.S. in chemistry there in 1963.

She began working for the Oklahoma Medical Research Foundation and moved up to a research position as a chemist. She met her future husband, also a chemist, when he turned her down for a job. But Michael Lucid kept her in mind and when a job opened up that he thought was right for her, he called her up to offer it to her. She took the job and eventually married Mike.

She and Mike had two daughters, and then Shannon decided to go back to school. She received her Ph.D. in biochemistry from the University of Oklahoma in 1973, the same year she had her son.

As both a chemist and a science fiction buff, Lucid was fascinated by the idea of space exploration and life forms in outer space. Before she married Mike, Shannon had talked to him about her desire to become an astronaut and they both agreed that she should apply. In 1977, she learned that NASA was looking for more astronauts. She applied and was accepted. Mike and the children are very excited about Shannon's involvement in the space program.

The jump from researcher to astronaut may seem like a big one, but Shannon Lucid has loved flying ever since she was five years old. She has a commercial pilot's license and over 1500 hours of flying time. One of her early career choices would have been to be an airline pilot, but the airlines were not hiring women pilots in the early 1960s. It's not surprising that her favorite part of astronaut training was flying in the T-38 trainer jet.

Bonnie Dunbar sits in the rear seat of the T-38 trainer jet. As an astronaut, she finally achieved her dream of jet flight.

Mission 51-J: Bonnie Dunbar

The space shuttle *Challenger* soared into orbit on Wednesday, October 30, 1985, at 11:00 A.M. CST. The largest crew ever included mission specialist Bonnie Dunbar.

The astronauts split into two groups of four each. Working in 12-hour shifts, they conducted 40 experiments in the pressurized *Spacelab*. The astronauts tested the processing of certain materials, grew some crystals, observed the behavior of liquids in weightlessness, tended a small garden, monitored the growth of South African frog larvae, and tested a device to precisely locate *Challenger*'s position in space.

Challenger landed at Edwards Air Force Base on November 6, 1985.

Growing up on a farm in the state of Washington, Bonnie Dunbar has felt close to the stars all her life. As a young girl in the late 1950s, she used to gaze into the night sky, longing to explore that vast unknown. At that time she wanted to be a jet pilot. *Astronaut* was an unknown word.

Dunbar's parents, who had homesteaded their land in 1948 to build their wheat farm, told her that she could do anything she wanted. Dunbar's mother wanted her oldest child to be the first in the family to get a college degree.

The nearest town was several miles away, so Dunbar had few playmates aside from her family. She spent a lot of time reading. Her favorite books were the classics and science fiction. Her high school physics teacher encouraged Dunbar to use her strengths in math and science to major in engineering.

The crew of mission 61-A was the largest ever to occupy an orbiting spacecraft at the same time. In front are West German payload specialist Reinhard Furrer, mission specialists Bonnie Dunbar and James Buchli, and commander Henry Hartsfield, Jr. In back are pilot Steven Nagel, mission specialist Guion Bluford, and payload specialists Ernst Messerschmid of West Germany and Wubbo Ockels of the Netherlands.

Since her first choice for a college was too expensive and her second choice did not accept women as students in 1967, Dunbar went to the University of Washington. What excited her about enrolling at the University was that they had been asked to develop a heat protection system for the space shuttle. This gave her the chance to take part in the earliest research on the tiles that would be used to protect the space shuttle during reentry. She never told anyone that one day she hoped to be *on* the shuttle.

She worked for Boeing Computer Services for a time, and then went for postgraduate work at the University of Illinois. Next, Rockwell International hired her to help set up production of the space shuttle tiles in California.

In 1977, she applied for the job of mission specialist/astronaut with NASA, but she was not accepted. She realized she needed to broaden her background, so she took a job with NASA which let her work with people instead of machines. Her job as a systems engineer was to take complicated engineering concepts, break them down into simpler ideas, and help communicate them to people in other technical areas of NASA.

Two years later, she reapplied to the astronaut program and was accepted. During her training at NASA she also attended the University of Houston and earned a Ph.D. in biomedical engineering. Her specialty was studying how well human beings survive in space for extended time periods.

Dunbar's dream of jet flight also came true. Like the other astronaut trainees, she spent about 15 hours per month rocketing at up to 800 mph (1280 kph) in NASA's T-38s.

Dunbar also spent many hours in the classroom learning star identification, geology, astrophysics, and more about the science of flight. She was co-anchor with Dan Rather during CBS's coverage of the second flight of *Columbia*.

Bonnie Dunbar is enthusiastic about the shuttle program. She talks about the satellites launched each year as big business. She told one reporter, "What we need now is a space station. A space operations center would allow us to do some of the best earth observations of weather, crops, and oceans, as well as service repair of vehicles. It's going to happen, and it's not going to help us economically to ask the Japanese or Europeans to do the launching for us." It's exciting to listen to Bonnie Dunbar as she talks about building space furnaces that can be used to make new kinds of alloys and crystals, and about outer space transportation becoming commonplace. Sometimes science fiction doesn't stay in the realm of fiction—it becomes a reality.

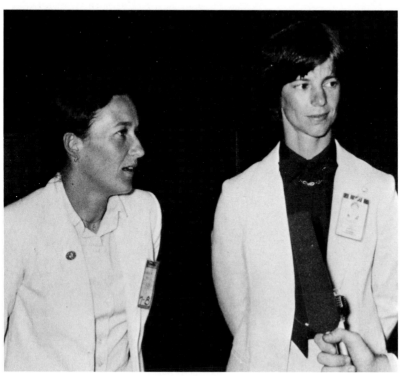

Meeting the press is an important part of an astronaut's job. Mary Cleave (left) and Bonnie Dunbar give an interview.

61

Above: The crew of 61-B included payload specialist Charles Walker, commander Brewster Shaw, and mission specialists Jerry L. Ross, Mary Cleave, and Sherwood Spring, pilot Bryan O'Connor, and payload specialist Rodolfo Neri of Mexico. **Right:** Jerry Ross perches on the RMS beside the structure he and Spring have just built in space.

Mission 61-B: Mary Cleave

Stars were visible as the crew of mission 61-B boarded their new orbiter, *Atlantis*. Only two of the crew members, payload specialist Charles Walker and commander Brewster Shaw, had ever been into space before. For the rest, including mission specialist Mary Cleave, it was the first trip into space.

On November 26, 1985, at 7:29 P.M. EST, *Atlantis* and its seven crew members rose steadily into the heavens. Mary Cleave functioned as the flight engineer for the launch. About 2 hours and 40 minutes after launch, when the flight was well underway, Cleave began a series of experiments for the 3M Corporation.

Walker then began experiments to make erythropoietin, a red blood cell stimulant, and to grow protein crystals large enough so that he could determine their three-dimensional atomic structures. This would help scientists develop powerful new medicines.

On November 7, *Atlantis* deployed a Mexican communications satellite, *Morelos-B*, and an Australian communications satellite, *Aussat*. The Australians paid NASA $9.5 million for deploying their satellite—satellites are big business for the space program.

The highlight of the mission, however, was the 12 hours that astronauts Sherwood Spring and Jerry Ross spent working outside *Atlantis*. They built the first large structures in space. NASA timed them and they reported their progress to Houston. Their experience would help NASA plan the construction of a permanent space station. In just 55 minutes they built a 45-foot (13.5-m) tower. With Ross riding on the end of the manipulator arm, Cleave maneuvered him into position so that he could fit the more than 100 pieces together to make the tower. Then, drifting in space with only a safety wire holding them to the shuttle, the two men built a pyramid structure in space. Spring reported that his hands were tired and his fingers starting to get numb as they finished their construction. This first EVA lasted 5 hours and 30 minutes. Both men reported being tired.

Ross and Spring began their second EVA on December 1, 1985. They practiced building and dismantling the tower and the pyramid structure seven more times during this EVA. *Atlantis* flew into darkness over the Atlantic and Cleave repositioned Ross so that he could lift the entire 45-foot structure. Spring had already released the supports holding it to *Atlantis*. Ross brought the tower back onto the supports with ease. Then photographs were taken of Spring holding the huge tower while standing atop the RMS. He showed that he could reposition the tower. This second EVA lasted six and a half hours.

The crew spent two more days in orbit before touching down on December 3, 1985, at Edwards Air Force Base.

Mary Cleave did not always want to be an astronaut. In fact, when the Russians sent a dog into space in the late 1950s, she was horrified. She had a little beagle and the thought of sending him so far from home seemed incredibly cruel.

In spite of her feelings for the dog, Mary Cleave has always been interested in flying. When she was young, she went to an air show at an air force base. She climbed into the cockpit of one of the jets and felt she was in heaven. She said aloud how much she wanted to fly a jet, and she was told, "You'll never fly one of these, young lady."

So she saved up her money and, with the help of her parents, earned her pilot's license. Her mother would drive her to the airport, and then Cleave would take her mother up in a plane.

Cleave wanted to be an airline cabin attendant, but at five feet one and a half inches (154 cm), she was too short. She loved nature, and when she first went to college she wanted to become a large-animal veterinarian. But after two years, she realized that she was too small for that, too. So she got her degree from Colorado State University in biology, intending to teach as her mother did.

Her first teaching job was on a "floating campus," a ship full of college kids which sailed around the oceans. Cleave taught biology, but she also began some research into ecology and pollution. She took samples of water wherever the ship stopped and analyzed the samples for pollutants.

In 1971, she went back to school at Utah State University to study *phycology*, or the science of algae. She

Mary Cleave has taken her turn here in Mission Control at Houston, acting as capcom for a mission.

got a job in the Utah Water Research Laboratory, which analyzes sewers and pollution. She was one of the few women there, and she saw that most of the men in the lab were certified engineers. So she went on to get doctorates in civil and aeronautical engineering.

One day in 1978, a co-worker tossed a NASA brochure on her desk, joking that she was the only one in the lab crazy enough to want to be an astronaut. Mary Cleave applied right away, but she was turned down.

Two years later, she applied again. NASA asked her to come to Houston for interviews and tests. She looked around Johnson Space Center. She fell asleep when they zipped her up inside the rescue ball to test for claustrophobia. She answered all of the psychologists' questions (when they asked how long she had wanted to be an astronaut, she said, "Are you serious? . . . I thought you guys would never take women into the program."). And then, to her joy, she was accepted.

Cleave's first assignment for NASA was a design for a new space toilet for the shuttle. She has also taken her turn at the job of capcom.

Cleave says that she wants to be in the space program because she believes that it will give humankind some valuable benefits, such as the production of new drugs. She finds the space program's potential to improve the quality of life important and exciting.

Marsha Ivins

Ellen Shulman

Kathryn Thornton

Linda Godwin

The Dream Continues

Marsha Ivins finished her astronaut training in 1985. She holds a number of pilot's licenses and ratings, for everything from multiengine airline transports to gliders. Ivins is a member of the Flying 99s (the International Women Pilots Association), the Soaring Society of America, Experimental Aircraft Association, and International Aerobatic Club.

She has worked at the Johnson Space Center since July 1974. Ivins has worked on orbiter displays and controls and human/machine engineering, and as flight simulation engineer on the shuttle training aircraft.

Ivins holds a degree in aerospace engineering from the University of Colorado. She was born on April 15, 1951, in Baltimore, Maryland.

Ellen Shulman is another of the class of '85. Her father is a medical doctor, and Shulman chose the same vocation for herself. She received her M.D. from Cornell University in 1978. She also has an undergraduate degree in geology.

Born on April 17, 1953, in Fayetteville, North Carolina, her recreational interests include swimming, skiing, running, softball, movies, music, and reading.

During her three-year residency after medical school, she specialized in internal medicine (treating diseases that do not need surgery). In 1981, Shulman joined NASA as a medical officer at the Johnson Space Center. At the time she was selected for the astronaut program, she was working as a physician in the Flight Medicine Clinic.

Kathryn Thornton became a full astronaut in 1985. Dr. Thornton holds a B.S. in physics from Auburn University, and M.S. and Ph.D. degrees in physics from the University of Virginia. During graduate school she worked on nuclear physics research programs at Oak Ridge National Laboratory, Brookhaven National Laboratory, Indiana University Cyclotron Facility, and the Space Radiation Effects Laboratory. In 1980 she took a job as a physicist at the United States Army Foreign Science and Technology Center. She was working there when she became an astronaut-trainee.

Thornton is married to Stephen Thornton, Ph.D., who has two children from a previous marriage. Stephen and Kathryn have a young daughter, Carol. Stephen Thornton teaches physics at the University of Virginia. He flies to Houston every month to visit his wife and daughter.

Linda Godwin is one of two women who began their training in 1985 and became full astronauts in 1986. Born on July 2, 1952, Godwin is from Cape Girardeau, Missouri. With a Ph.D. in physics from the University of Missouri, she was working at Johnson Space Center as a payload officer when selected for the astronaut program.

Tamara Jernigan is the other woman admitted in 1985. Born on May 7, 1959, in Chattanooga, Tennessee, the young astronaut is a physicist, pilot, astrophysicist, athlete, and chef. At Stanford University, Jernigan played varsity volleyball and earned a B.S.

Tammy Jernigan

in physics. She also received her master's degree in aeronautics (the study of designing and operating aircraft) from Stanford.

While in college, Jernigan worked summers as a technical aide in NASA's Jet Propulsion Lab in Pasadena, California. When selected as an astronaut candidate she was working on her doctorate in astronomy and was a research scientist at NASA's Ames Research Center at Moffett Field, California.

In Memoriam: Challenger, *January 28, 1986*

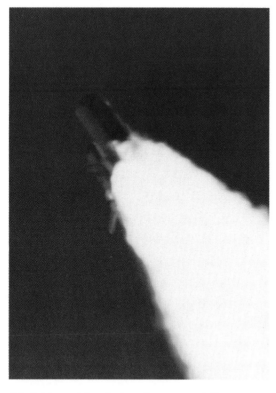

A bright, sustained glow becomes visible on the side of *Challenger* just before the explosion.

January 28, 1986, is a date that will never be forgotten by any astronaut. It was a very chilly morning for Florida. The nighttime temperature had fallen to 27° F (-2° C) and by sunrise was just above freezing. Mission 51-L had been delayed twice due to poor weather conditions but today it looked as if they would finally launch.

Friends and family cheered as commander Francis Scobee, pilot Michael Smith, mission specialists Judith Resnik, Ronald McNair, and Ellison Onizuka, and payload specialists Christa McAuliffe, a high school teacher, and Gregory Jarvis, a civilian engineer, stepped confidently into the launch area. Resnik, the flight engineer, took her seat on the upper deck with the pilot and commander. The other four crew members strapped themselves into seats on the mid-deck.

Like any explorers, the crew realized that there was an element of danger in their flight. They knew they were sitting on three enormous tanks of fuel that, once ignited, could only continue to burn until their fuel was spent. Most people not involved with NASA pushed that fact aside, however. Few people could have imagined that, soon after lift-off, *Challenger* would suffer a "malfunction"—an explosion that ended its journey and the lives of its crew.

Seventy-three seconds into the flight, an immense explosion stunned those watching from the launch pad. The solid rocket boosters broke away from the *Challenger*, still flaming as they fell to the sea. At the time, all the NASA commentator could say was, "Flight controllers here looking very carefully at the situation. Obviously,

a major malfunction." Only 73 seconds after lift-off, the flight was over. All seven crew members were killed.

Investigators have decided that the cause of the explosion was a mechanical malfunction. A seal between sections of the right booster leaked because it had gotten too cold the night before and had not yet warmed up at the time of launch. This leaking seal allowed flames to shoot out the side of the booster, flames which burned through into the liquid fuel tank. The liquid fuel tank exploded.

NASA recovered pieces of the shuttle and studied them along with all of the data the shuttle's computers and sensors recorded during the flight. The booster rockets have been redesigned and retested.

The *Challenger* crew: front row, Michael J. Smith, Francis R. (Dick) Scobee, and Ronald E. McNair; back row, Ellison S. Onizuka, Sharon Christa McAuliffe, Gregory Jarvis, and Judith A. Resnik

Christa McAuliffe enjoyed her training immensely and was looking forward to teaching about space from space.

In addition, NASA and a special commission of Congress examined the way in which NASA decided to go ahead with the launch in spite of the cold. They asked who made the decisions and whose advice was listened to. The result of this investigation was that some people at NASA were fired, and some of the methods for deciding whether to launch were changed. It was a costly lesson in human life, materials, and time. All shuttle flights were stopped for over two years.

Christa McAuliffe, when chosen to be the first teacher in space, told reporters that even though she had only one body, there would be 10 souls up there with her. She meant the 10 finalists of the teacher-in-space program, but *Challenger's* crew took many more souls than that with them

when they died. For many people, McAuliffe symbolized the chance that ordinary people, not just Ph.D.s or pilots, could go into space. Millions of students were ready to have Mc-Auliffe explain to them how the shuttle works and what the benefits and history of space travel are. No doubt she would still think the benefits outweigh the costs.

Before he boarded the shuttle, Scobee expressed a belief that the future of humankind depends on space exploration. He would want the United States space program to go on.

So, too, would Judith Resnik. She said that she had never been happier than since becoming an astronaut. Her love of learning would cause her to urge those she left behind to continue space exploration.

Above: The Canadian space team includes Bob Thirsk, Steve MacLean, and Marc Garneau (in front), and Ken Money, Roberta Bondar, and Bjarni Tryggvason (in back). **Below:** Japanese payload specialists: Mamoru Mohri, Chiaki Naito, and Takao Doi

Astronauts from Outside the United States

Canada's Team

Canada's astronaut team is based at the National Research Council in Ottawa. All of the 1988 team trained as payload specialists. NASA does not require payload specialists to go through the same training program as its astronauts. Marc Garneau flew on mission 41-G and Bob Thirsk acted as backup. Roberta Bondar is the first woman on the Canadian team.

Because they are all payload specialists, the Canadian astronauts are training to become experts on the experiments that Canada sends on the space shuttle. They also visit the aviation medicine facilities in Montreal and Toronto. At these facilities, they become familiar with the effects of high altitude flight and motion sickness. They practice using the equipment that they will be using in flight.

The emblem for the Canadian space team

In addition, the crew becomes familiar, in a general way, with the shuttle systems. They all make several visits to the Johnson Space Center

73

and the Kennedy Space Center. Two months before a flight, the payload specialist and backup person report back to Johnson Space Center for lectures and demonstrations involving shuttle system trainers. They also undergo the experience of zero gravity by flying on the KC-135 jet, and they participate in mission simulations. The entire crew for a particular shuttle flight works together every day for the week before launch. The pilot, commander, and mission specialists, however, work together periodically for a whole year to learn their roles.

Roberta Bondar, the first female member of the team, comes from Sault Ste. Marie, Ontario. She was born there on December 4, 1945.

Bondar holds bachelor's degrees in zoology and agriculture, a doctorate in neurobiology, and a doctor of medicine degree. Apparently this has not kept her busy enough, because she has also become an excellent pilot. Bondar is a member of the 99s (International Women Pilots Association), the Canadian Owners and Pilots Association, and the Canadian Society of Aviation Medicine.

Japan's Team

In August 1985, the National Space Development Agency (NASDA) in Tokyo, Japan, selected Japan's first team of astronauts. One of the three was a woman, and one of these astronauts will fly aboard the shuttle in 1989 or 1990.

The NASDA expects to recruit 10 more astronauts by 1993. Some of them will work aboard the new United States space station.

Tsukuba Science City, 40 miles (64 km) northeast of Tokyo, is where most of NASDA's preparations for human space flight take place. This city of 142,000 is dedicated exclusively to science and technology development. Tsukuba Space Center is similar to Johnson Space Center in that it is Japan's main satellite control center. Space experiments are designed there, and it is where Japanese spacecraft are tested. The space center has a large chamber that scientists and engineers can use to simulate a space environment for satellite tests. Launches are performed at the Tanegashima Space Center in southern Japan, but flights are controlled from Tsukuba after the first 30 minutes.

Chiaki Naito is the only woman in the first astronaut group. Naito is a heart specialist at the Keio University Medical School outside Tokyo.

A Look at the Future

The future for women scientists in the space program is exciting. Every group of astronauts chosen since 1977 has included women and there is no reason to expect this to change. Whether one is male or female is no longer important to NASA. Women who put in the long hours necessary for a career in the sciences can share in the challenge of exploration and discovery that working in the space program can bring. Perhaps the next time "mankind" steps on the soil of another heavenly body, women will lead the way.

An exciting development for the future is the Space Telescope (ST). ST will take up most of the shuttle's cargo bay, but once it is launched it will let scientists view the heavens without the distortion of the earth's atmosphere. Its powerful lens will enable astronomers to see into the center of far-off galaxies. This may help scientists understand how galaxies began. Astronomers from all over the world may have their questions answered with ST's help.

Another future possibility is the development of an unpiloted space vehicle that can lift as much as 200,000 pounds (90,000 kg). Such a vehicle would make it possible to build a permanent space station more quickly. The operation of a permanent space station will mean jobs for even more astronauts in the future.

A permanent space station is in NASA's plans for the 1990s, but planning goes beyond that. Sally Ride prepared a report for NASA, released in August 1987, in which she discussed

Above: Space Telescope will be launched from the shuttle and will let astronomers see much farther than they can from any telescope on earth. **Left:** The space station will have laboratories and living quarters in the center and solar panels at each end.

the space program and made recommendations about its future. One of her recommendations was that the United States establish an outpost on the moon. This would give astronauts experience and information needed for an expedition to Mars—an expedition which might include both cosmonauts and astronauts again.

Perhaps you will be on one of these missions of the future.

You Can Be an Astronaut Now

There is a place where you can learn more about space and experience being an "astronaut" for a week. United States Space Camp in Huntsville, Alabama, is a summer camp for grade school and high school students. Operated by the Alabama Space and Rocket Center, space camp lets you learn about the science of rocketry and what it is like to work in the space program and fly on the shuttle. You may even meet a shuttle astronaut or two. In just five days, campers build small rockets that really fly, build a structure while under water, work in *Spacelab*, and become part of a simulated shuttle mission.

In order to find out more about space camp, contact:

Edward O. Buckbee
United States Space Camp
The Space and Rocket Center
Tranquility Base
Huntsville, AL 35807
Telephone: 1-800-633-7280

Space campers can use shuttle and mission control mockups during a simulated mission.

Space Talk

astronaut: a person who flies into space

capsule communicator or **capcom:** an astronaut in Mission Control on the ground who talks to the astronauts in space

cargo bay: the large section of the orbiter that holds large equipment such as satellites

commander: the shuttle crew member responsible for the success and safety of the flight who controls the shuttle during launch, reentry, and in-flight maneuvers

cosmonaut: a Soviet astronaut

deploy: to place something into proper position; to remove something from the cargo bay of an orbiting shuttle and set it into space

dock: to join one vehicle with another in space

extravehicular activity (EVA): an astronaut's activities outside the shuttle in space; also called a *space walk*.

flight engineer: the crew member responsible for the mechanical performance of the aircraft

G: a unit of force, equal to the force of gravity on a body at rest on earth and used to indicate the force of acceleration

getaway special: canister aboard the shuttle containing an experiment designed by a high school or college student

Mission Control: the people in a space center who direct the activities of astronauts in space

mission simulator: a model of the shuttle's cabin which stays on the ground but can be made to seem as though it is taking off or flying. Astronauts practice "flying" in it under different conditions. Sometimes called a *shuttle simulator*.

mission specialist: astronaut trained to work with payloads, not to pilot the shuttle

orbiter: the shuttle itself without its rocket boosters and fuel tank

payload: all of the cargo, including scientific equipment to be used for experiments, carried into space by a spacecraft

payload specialist: a person familiar with the payload on the shuttle, not trained as an astronaut

pilot: a person who can fly the shuttle and is backup to the commander

reentry: the return to the earth's atmosphere after travel in space

remote manipulator system or **RMS:** a robotic arm in the orbiter's cargo bay and its controls inside the shuttle. It allows astronauts to manipulate items in the cargo bay without leaving the shuttle.

solid rocket booster: one of two rockets filled with solid fuel which provide extra power to the shuttle during launch

space: officially, the area more than 50 miles above the earth's surface where there is no atmosphere

thrust: a forward or upward push made by gases escaping through the rear of the rocket engines

vernier engine: a small engine used to adjust speed and direction

zero gravity or **zero G:** the condition of no gravity or weightlessness in space

Index

Numbers in **bold** refer to photographs.

ACKNOWLEDGEMENTS
All photographs in this book courtesy of NASA except for the following: pp. 24, 28, Tass from Sovfoto; pp. 26, 27 (top), UPI/Bettmann Newsphotos; pp. 27 (bottom), 30, Novosti Press Agency; pp. 72 (top), 73, National Research Council of Canada; p. 72 (bottom), National Space Development Agency (NASDA) of Japan; p. 77, Bob Gathany/U.S. Space Camp.
The cover photograph is courtesy of NASA.